Gooseberry Patch Co.

Our Favorite
Money-Saving
Recipes

Copyright 2010, Gooseberry Patch
First Printing, March, 2010

The secret to serving a hearty homestyle meal on
a busy weeknight! Simply prepare a favorite casserole recipe
the night before, cover and refrigerate. Just add 15 to
20 extra minutes to the baking time.

Italian Supper Casserole

1-1/2 lbs. ground beef
1 onion, chopped
1 green pepper, sliced
28-oz. can crushed tomatoes
1-1/2 c. water
1 T. dried oregano

salt and pepper to taste
8-oz. pkg. wide egg noodles,
   cooked and divided
1 c. shredded Cheddar cheese
4-oz. can sliced mushrooms,
   drained

In a skillet over medium heat, brown ground beef with onion; drain. Add green pepper; cook until tender. Add tomatoes, water, oregano, salt and pepper, stirring often. Remove from heat. Spread half the noodles in a greased 13"x9" baking pan; layer half the ground beef mixture on top. Sprinkle with half the cheese; repeat layers. Spread mushrooms on top. Bake, uncovered, at 350 degrees for 20 to 30 minutes.

Give store brands a try for canned veggies, soups and sauces, boxed baking mixes and other pantry staples! You'll find they usually taste just as good as famous-label items and save you money too.

Easy Mac & Cheese   *Makes 4 to 6 servings*

2 c. elbow macaroni, uncooked   10-3/4 oz. can cream of
2 c. milk   mushroom soup
2 c. Cheddar cheese, cubed   1/4 c. onion, chopped

Combine all ingredients in a greased 2-quart casserole dish. Bake one
hour at 350 degrees, uncovered, stirring once during baking.

Meatloaf is so easy to fix, and everybody loves it! Why not
double the recipe and save half, then serve up meatloaf
sandwiches for another quick & easy meal.

Just Like Mom's Meatloaf

2 eggs, beaten
8-oz. can tomato sauce
3/4 c. cracker crumbs
1/4 c. onion, chopped
1/4 c. green pepper, finely
     chopped
1 T. Worcestershire sauce

1 t. salt
1/2 t. pepper
1-1/2 lbs. ground beef
1/2 c. catsup
2 t. mustard
2 T. brown sugar, packed

Combine first 8 ingredients in a large bowl; add ground beef and mix well. Shape into a loaf; place in an ungreased 9"x5" loaf pan. Bake at 350 degrees for one hour. Combine catsup, mustard and brown sugar; pour over meatloaf and bake an additional 10 to 15 minutes.

Simmering chicken to use later in casseroles? Let it cool in its broth before cutting or shredding...it'll have twice the flavor.

Chilly-Day Chicken Pot Pie

Serves 4

2 9-inch pie crusts
1/4 c. margarine
1/4 c. all-purpose flour
1/4 t. poultry seasoning
1/8 t. pepper

1 c. chicken broth
2/3 c. milk
2 c. cooked chicken, cubed
2 c. frozen mixed vegetables,
   thawed

Place one crust in an ungreased 9" pie plate; set aside. Melt margarine in a saucepan over medium heat; stir in flour, seasoning and pepper. Cook and stir until mixture is smooth and bubbly. Gradually add broth and milk; bring to a boil. Reduce heat and simmer, stirring constantly until mixture thickens. Stir in chicken and vegetables; cook until heated through. Pour into pie plate. Place second crust over filling; crimp edges and cut vents in top. Bake at 400 degrees for 20 to 30 minutes, until golden.

When the weather is nice, carry dinner outdoors to the backyard for a picnic. You'll be making memories together...and just about everything seems to taste even better outdoors!

One-Pot Pork Chop Supper

1 T. butter
4 boneless pork chops,
   1/2-inch thick
3 redskin potatoes, quartered
2 c. baby carrots

1 onion, quartered
10-3/4 oz. can cream of
   mushroom soup
1/4 c. water

Melt butter in a large skillet over medium heat. Add pork chops; sauté 3 minutes per side, or until golden. Add potatoes, carrots and onion. In a small bowl, combine soup and water; pour over pork chops. Cover and simmer for 15 to 20 minutes, or until pork chops are done and vegetables are tender.

Freezing cheese causes it to turn crumbly...ideal in baked casserole dishes! So when cheese goes on sale, stock up and fill the freezer. Thaw cheese in the fridge and use within a few days.

Pizza Mac & Cheese

Makes 8 servings

7-1/4 oz. pkg. macaroni
    & cheese
2 eggs, beaten

16-oz. jar pizza sauce
4-oz. pkg. sliced pepperoni
1 c. shredded mozzarella cheese

Prepare macaroni and cheese according to package directions; remove from heat. Add eggs; mix well. Pour into a greased 13"x9" baking pan. Bake, uncovered, at 375 degrees for 10 minutes. Spread with pizza sauce; layer pepperoni and mozzarella cheese on top. Return to oven until cheese melts, about 10 minutes. Cut into squares.

A thrifty tip...try using a little less ground beef in tried & true recipes. Add a few more veggies or a little more pasta... chances are good that no one will even notice!

Chuck Wagon Casserole

Makes 6 servings

1 lb. lean ground beef
1/2 c. onion, chopped
1/2 c. green pepper, chopped
15-1/2 oz. can mild chili beans
   in sauce

3/4 c. barbecue sauce
1/2 t. salt
8-1/2 oz. pkg. cornbread mix
11-oz. can sweet corn & diced
   peppers, drained

In a frying pan over medium heat, cook beef, onion and pepper; stir until no longer pink. Drain. Stir in chili beans, barbecue sauce and salt; bring to a boil. Spoon into a lightly greased 13"x9" baking pan and set aside. Prepare cornbread mix according to package directions; stir in corn and spoon over meat mixture. Bake at 400 degrees for 30 minutes, or until golden.

Include family members in meal planning, grocery shopping and cooking. Picky eaters are much more likely to eat food that they've chosen and cooked themselves!

Zippy Chicken Fingers

Serves 4

4 boneless, skinless chicken
    breasts, cut into strips
juice of 1 lemon
poultry seasoning to taste
1-1/2 c. seasoned dry bread
    crumbs

1/4 c. oil
Optional: honey mustard or
    barbecue sauce

Place chicken strips in a bowl; sprinkle with lemon juice, then with
poultry seasoning to taste. Spread bread crumbs in a shallow dish;
coat each chicken strip with crumbs. Spread oil in a 13"x9" baking
pan; arrange strips on top. Bake, uncovered, at 375 degrees for
20 minutes, turning once, until cooked through and golden. Serve
with dipping sauces, if desired.

Thank God for dirty dishes,
They have a tale to tell.
While others may go hungry,
We're eating very well.

~ Author Unknown

Skillet Supper

Serves 4

1-1/2 T. butter
3 potatoes, peeled, thinly sliced
   and divided
1/2 c. green onions, chopped
   and divided
1/2 c. green pepper, chopped
   and divided

2 c. cooked ham, diced
1/2 t. salt
pepper to taste
3 eggs, beaten
1/2 c. shredded Cheddar
   cheese

Melt butter in a skillet over medium heat; layer with half of the vegetables and ham. Sprinkle with salt and pepper; repeat layers. Cover and cook until potatoes are tender, about 20 to 25 minutes; pour eggs on top. Cover and cook until set, about 17 minutes. Uncover and sprinkle with cheese. Cover and heat until cheese is melted; cut into wedges to serve.

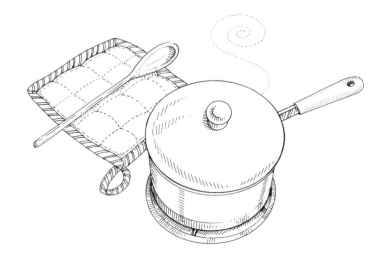

Save odds & ends of leftover veggies in
a freezer bag...before you know it, you'll have enough
for a big pot of hearty soup!

Mom's Vegetable Soup

Makes 12 to 14 servings

6 c. water
7 potatoes, peeled and chopped
1/2 head cabbage, shredded
1 to 2 onions, chopped
16-oz. can mixed vegetables
16-oz. can peas, drained

2 8-oz. cans tomato sauce
1-1/2 c. elbow macaroni,
  uncooked
1/2 c. bacon drippings
2 t. salt
1 t. pepper

Place water in a 5-quart stockpot over high heat. Add potatoes, cabbage and onions; bring to a rolling boil. Reduce heat; cover and simmer for 10 minutes, or until potatoes are tender. Stir in remaining ingredients; add more water as needed to fill pot. Return to a rolling boil. Simmer, covered, for 20 minutes, or until soup is thickened and macaroni is tender. Add additional salt and pepper to taste.

Cooking in aluminum foil is a fun way to prepare an all-in-one meal the whole family will love. Be sure to select heavy-duty aluminum foil...and watch out for escaping hot steam when you open the package!

King-of-the-Road Dinner

Serves 4

4 carrots, peeled and sliced
6 potatoes, peeled and sliced
1 onion, sliced
1/2 head cabbage, sliced

10-3/4 oz. can cream of
  mushroom soup
1 to 2 lbs. Kielbasa, cut into
  bite-size slices

Arrange vegetables in an aluminum foil grilling pouch sprayed with non-stick vegetable spray. Spoon soup over vegetables; top with Kielbasa. Seal pouch tightly; set in a shallow baking pan and place on heated grill. Grill for 30 minutes; turn pouch over and grill for an additional 30 minutes. Pouch may also be placed on a baking sheet and baked at 450 degrees for 30 to 45 minutes.

Stir up a dilly of a sauce for salmon patties. Whisk together
1/2 cup sour cream, one tablespoon Dijon mustard, one tablespoon
lemon juice and 2 teaspoons chopped fresh dill.
Chill...so simple and so good!

Quick Salmon Patties

Serves 6

2 14-3/4 oz. cans salmon,
    bones removed
1 onion, chopped
30 saltine crackers, crushed

3 eggs
1/8 t. pepper
1/8 t. salt
Optional: 6 sandwich buns, split

Spray a skillet with non-stick vegetable spray. Combine all ingredients except buns in a mixing bowl. Form into 6 patties. Place in skillet; cook over medium heat until lightly golden on each side. Serve on buns, if desired.

Take time to share family stories and traditions with your kids! A cherished family recipe can be a great conversation starter at dinner.

Grandma's Meatballs & Sauce

Serves 4

1 lb. ground beef
5-oz. can evaporated milk
1/2 c. onion, chopped
3/4 c. quick-cooking oats,
    uncooked
salt and pepper to taste
1 c. catsup

2 T. Worcestershire sauce
2 T. brown sugar, packed
1 T. vinegar
1/2 c. water
Optional: 4 hard rolls, split,
    or cooked pasta

Mix together ground beef, evaporated milk, onion, oats, salt and pepper; roll into one-inch balls. Brown in a skillet for 2 to 4 minutes; place in an ungreased 13"x9" baking pan. Set aside. Combine catsup, Worcestershire sauce, sugar, vinegar and water; pour over meatballs. Bake, uncovered, at 350 degrees for one hour. To serve, spoon into hard rolls or over pasta.

Turn leftover bits & pieces of cheese from the fridge into
a scrumptious sandwich topping. Just shred cheese and
stir in enough mayo to make a spreadable consistency. Serve
on crusty bread...yum!

BBQ Beef Sandwiches

Makes 6 servings

1-1/2 lbs. ground beef
1 T. mustard
1 c. catsup
1 T. vinegar

4 T. sugar
2 T. onion, diced
6 sandwich buns, split

Brown beef in a skillet over medium heat. Drain; add remaining ingredients except buns. Simmer for 15 minutes, stirring occasionally. Serve on sandwich buns.

Don't toss that almost-empty pickle jar...make tangy marinated veggies in a jiffy! Just add cut-up cucumbers, green peppers, carrots, cauliflower and other favorite fresh veggies to the remaining pickle juice and refrigerate. Enjoy within a few days.

Turkey Club Bake

2 c. biscuit baking mix
1/2 c. mayonnaise, divided
1/3 c. milk
2 c. cooked turkey, cubed
2 green onions, sliced

6 slices bacon, crisply cooked
  and crumbled
1 tomato, chopped
2/3 c. shredded Colby Jack
  cheese

Combine biscuit mix, 1/3 cup mayonnaise and milk until a soft dough forms; press into a 12"x8" rectangle. Arrange on a lightly buttered baking sheet; bake at 450 degrees until golden, about 8 to 10 minutes. Mix turkey, onions, bacon and remaining mayonnaise; spread over crust. Sprinkle with tomato and cheese; bake until cheese melts, about 5 to 6 minutes. Slice into squares to serve.

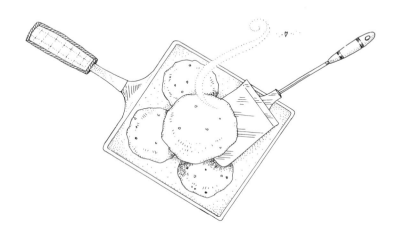

Crispy potato pancakes are a great way to use extra mashed potatoes. Stir an egg yolk and some minced onion into 2 cups potatoes. Form into patties and fry in a little oil until golden...yum!

Dressed-Up Dogs

Makes 4 sandwiches

8 hot dogs
8 slices rye bread
mayonnaise-type salad dressing
   to taste

Optional: mustard to taste
2 kosher dill pickles, sliced
   lengthwise
4 slices Swiss cheese

Slice hot dogs lengthwise, taking care not to cut all the way through. Arrange hot dogs cut-side down on a hot griddle sprayed with non-stick vegetable spray. Cook on each side until golden and warmed through; set aside. Spread 4 slices bread with salad dressing and mustard, if using; top each with 2 pickle spears, 2 hot dogs and one slice cheese. Top with remaining 4 slices bread.

Make-ahead freezer meals are like money in the bank!
Set aside a weekend each month to prepare several family-
pleasing dishes to tuck in the freezer. Why not invite a girlfriend
to help? You can both be filling your freezers while you
get caught up on the latest news.

Saucy Mozzarella Chicken

6 boneless, skinless chicken
   breasts
salt and pepper to taste
26-oz. jar spaghetti sauce

8-oz. pkg. shredded mozzarella
   cheese
Optional: cooked angel-hair
   pasta

Season chicken with salt and pepper; arrange in a greased
13"x9" baking pan. Pour spaghetti sauce on top. Bake, uncovered,
at 350 degrees for one hour and 10 minutes. Sprinkle with cheese;
return to oven until melted, an additional 5 to 10 minutes. Serve over
cooked pasta, if desired.

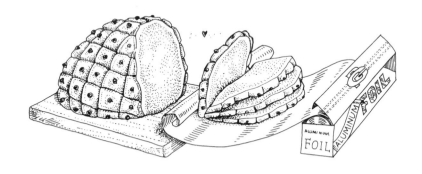

Ham is so versatile for whipping up scrumptious quick meals!
It's budget-friendly on supermarket holiday specials too. Why
not pick up an extra to cut into cubes or slices and freeze in
recipe-size portions. It'll be ready to add to casseroles
and egg dishes at a moment's notice.

Ham Steak & Brown Sugar Apples

Serves 4

2 T. butter
1/4 c. brown sugar, packed
2 T. country-style mustard

2 tart apples, cored and sliced
1-lb. ham steak

Melt butter in a skillet over medium heat, blend in brown sugar and mustard. Stir in apples and simmer until apples are just tender, 5 to 8 minutes. Spoon out apple mixture; set aside. Place ham steak in skillet and top with apple mixture. Cook, covered, until ham is heated through and done, 5 to 10 minutes.

When chopping onions or celery, it only takes a moment
to chop a little extra. Tuck them away in the freezer
for a quick start to dinner another day.

Unstuffed Pork Chops

Makes 4 servings

2 T. oil
4 thick pork chops
3 c. dry bread cubes or
    stuffing mix
1/4 c. butter, melted
1/4 c. chicken broth

2 T. celery, chopped
2 T. onion, chopped
1/4 t. poultry seasoning
10-3/4 oz. can cream of
    mushroom soup
1/3 c. water

In a large skillet, heat oil over medium heat; add pork chops and brown on both sides. Transfer to a lightly greased 13"x9" baking pan and set aside. Toss together bread cubes or stuffing, butter, broth, celery and onion in a large bowl. Spoon heaping mounds of bread crumb mixture over pork chops; set aside. Combine soup and water; pour over pork chops. Bake, covered, at 350 degrees for 30 minutes. Uncover and continue to bake for an additional 10 minutes, or until pork chops are cooked through.

Pour vegetable oil into a plastic squeeze bottle.
This makes it easy to drizzle oil just where it's needed,
with no waste and no mess.

Easy As 1-2-3 Chicken Bake

3/4 c. corn flake cereal, crushed
3/4 c. grated Parmesan cheese
1-oz. pkg. Italian salad dressing
   mix

8 boneless, skinless chicken
   breasts
1/3 c. margarine, melted

Mix cereal, Parmesan cheese and salad dressing mix together; coat chicken. Place in a single layer in a greased 13"x9" baking pan. Sprinkle any remaining cereal mixture on top; drizzle with butter. Bake, uncovered, at 350 degrees for 45 minutes, or until juices run clear when chicken is pierced with a fork.

Set a regular dinner theme for each night and it'll be a snap
to make out your shopping list. Some tasty, budget-friendly
themes are Spaghetti Night, Tex-Mex Night and
Leftovers night...your family is sure to think of others!

Mexican Cornbread Bake

Serves 4 to 6

1 lb. ground beef
4-1/2 oz. can chopped
   green chiles
1 onion, chopped
2 t. Mexican seasoning

1 T. chili powder
8-oz. can Mexican-style
   tomato sauce
8-1/2 oz. pkg. cornbread mix

In a skillet over medium heat, brown beef and drain. Add chiles, onion, seasoning and chili powder; cook until onion is tender. Add tomato sauce and simmer. Prepare cornbread batter according to package directions; pour half the batter into a lightly greased 2-quart baking dish. Spoon beef mixture over batter; top with remaining cornbread batter. Bake at 350 degrees for 25 to 30 minutes, or until cornbread is golden.

Invite the neighbors over for a casual dinner and let everyone
help in the preparations. What a terrific way to swap and try
new recipes...a budget-friendly way to entertain too!

Potato Puff Casserole

2 lbs. ground beef, browned
  and drained
10-3/4 oz. can cream of
  mushroom soup

32-oz. pkg. frozen potato
  puffs, thawed
Optional: shredded Cheddar
  cheese

Arrange ground beef in an ungreased 13"x9" baking pan. Spread
soup over beef; cover with potato puffs. Sprinkle with cheese,
if desired. Bake, uncovered, at 375 degrees for 20 to 30 minutes,
until heated through.

That man is richest whose pleasures are cheapest.

~ Henry David Thoreau

Skillet Surprise

Serves 4 to 6

1 to 2 T. olive oil
30-oz. pkg. frozen diced
    potatoes
1/2 onion, chopped
Optional: 1/2 green pepper,
    chopped

1 lb. beef, pork, sausage or
    other leftover cooked meat,
    chopped
8-oz. pkg. shredded Cheddar
    cheese

Heat oil in a large skillet over medium heat. Add potatoes, onion and pepper, if using; cook according to package directions. When potatoes are golden, add cooked meat; stir very well. Cover skillet; cook over low heat until heated through. Sprinkle with cheese; cover and let cheese melt.

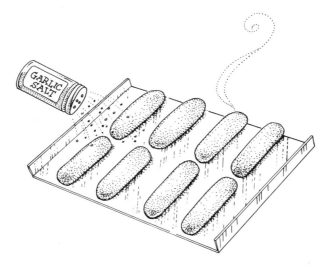

Turn leftover hamburger or hot dog buns into garlic bread
sticks in a jiffy! Spread with softened butter, sprinkle with
garlic salt and broil until toasty...yum!

Easy Chicken-Broccoli Alfredo

Serves 4

8-oz. pkg. linguine pasta,
   uncooked and divided
1 c. broccoli flowerets
10-3/4 oz. can cream of
   mushroom soup
1/2 c. milk

1/2 c. grated Parmesan cheese
1/4 t. pepper
2 c. cooked chicken, cubed
Garnish: grated Parmesan
   cheese

Cook half the package of linguine according to package directions,
reserving the rest for another recipe. Add broccoli during the last
4 minutes of cooking. Drain; keep warm. Mix soup, milk, cheese
and pepper in a saucepan; add chicken. Heat just until bubbly over
medium heat; spoon over cooked linguine. Serve with additional
Parmesan cheese.

Egg dishes like quiches, omelets and cheesy scrambled eggs
are just as yummy at dinnertime. Fresh eggs can safely be
refrigerated for 4 to 5 weeks, so go ahead and
stock up when they're on sale!

Ham & Cheddar Quiche

Serves 6 to 8

4 eggs, beaten
1 c. milk
1/4 t. salt
1/8 t. pepper

1 c. cooked ham, diced
8-oz. pkg. shredded sharp
     Cheddar cheese
9-inch deep-dish pie crust

Combine eggs, milk, salt, pepper, ham and cheese; mix well. Pour into pie crust. Bake at 350 degrees for 45 to 50 minutes.

Economical and quick-cooking, hot dogs and smoked sausage are great choices for weeknight meals. Different flavors like hickory-smoked or cheese-filled can really jazz up a recipe too.

Grandma's Hot Dog Skillet Meal

Serves 6

8-oz. pkg. medium egg noodles, uncooked and divided
6 hot dogs, sliced into 1/2-inch pieces
2 T. margarine
4 c. diced tomatoes

1 T. dried, minced onion
1/2 T. sugar
1/2 t. garlic powder
1/2 t. salt
Optional: grated Parmesan cheese

Cook half the noodles according to package directions; drain. Reserve remaining noodles for another recipe. In a large skillet over medium heat, brown hot dogs in margarine. Stir in cooked noodles and remaining ingredients except Parmesan cheese; bring to a boil. Reduce heat and simmer for 20 minutes, stirring occasionally. Sprinkle with Parmesan cheese, if desired.

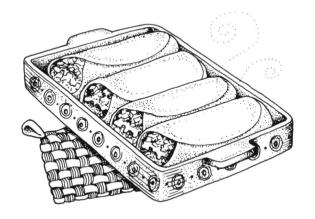

Turn leftover cooked chicken, beef or pork into the best-tasting enchiladas. Top flour tortillas with chopped meat, roll up and place in a baking pan. Cover with enchilada sauce and cheese, then bake until hot and bubbly. Serve with sour cream and guacamole...delicious!

Cheesy Corn & Bean Burritos

15-oz. can black beans, drained
  and rinsed
16-oz. can corn, drained
8-oz. can chopped green chiles,
  drained
12-oz. pkg. shredded Monterey
  Jack cheese, divided

Optional: 1 bunch fresh
  cilantro, divided
2 c. cooked rice
6 to 8 10-inch flour tortillas
16-oz. jar salsa, divided

Combine beans, corn, chiles, 2 cups cheese and 1/2 bunch chopped cilantro, if using; stir in cooked rice. Spoon 1/2 cup bean mixture along the center of each tortilla; top with 2 tablespoons salsa. Roll up burrito-style and arrange seam-side down in a greased 13"x9" baking pan. Spread any remaining bean mixture over burritos. Spoon remaining salsa over burritos and into corners of pan; top with remaining cheese. Cover loosely with aluminum foil. Bake at 425 degrees for 30 minutes, until heated through and cheese has melted. Garnish with remaining cilantro, if desired.

There's no better way to flavor foods than with fresh herbs...
you can even grow pots of herbs on the kitchen windowsill. Some
tasty ones to try are thyme, marjoram, chives and basil.

Perfect Cheesy Pasta Bake

Serves 4 to 6

16-oz. pkg. rotini pasta,
    uncooked and divided
3-1/2 c. spaghetti sauce
1/2 c. grated Parmesan cheese
1 c. cooked chicken, diced

1/2 c. shredded mozzarella
    cheese
1/2 c. shredded pasteurized
    process cheese spread

Measure out 4 cups uncooked pasta, reserving the rest for another recipe. Cook pasta as package directs; drain and place in a large bowl. Add spaghetti sauce and Parmesan cheese; mix well. Transfer half of pasta mixture into a greased 8"x8" baking pan. Add chicken; cover with remaining pasta mixture. Top with cheeses. Bake, uncovered, at 350 degrees for 30 to 35 minutes, until hot and bubbly.

Soups and stews are oh-so easy to extend when you need to feed a few more people. Just add a few more chopped veggies and a little more broth or tomato juice, then simmer until done...no one will know the difference!

Cheesy Chicken & Noodle Soup

Serves 6 to 8

2 to 3 c. chicken, cooked and
    shredded
10-3/4 oz. can Cheddar cheese
    soup
4 to 6 c. chicken broth

8-oz. pkg. fine egg noodles,
    uncooked
1 c. milk
Optional: shredded Cheddar
    cheese

Combine all ingredients except cheese in a large stockpot; bring to a boil over medium heat. Reduce heat; simmer until noodles are soft. Spoon into bowls; sprinkle with cheese, if desired.

Make a quick and hearty casserole with leftover chili. Start with about 4 cups of chili, add a can of corn and pour cornbread batter over everything. Top with a sprinkle of shredded cheese and bake for a filling (and tasty!) dinner.

Rich & Meaty Chili

Serves 6 to 8

1 lb. ground beef
1/2 c. onion, chopped
2 T. butter
2 15-1/2 oz. cans kidney beans
2 15-oz. cans chili beans
4 c. diced tomatoes
6-oz. can tomato paste
2 to 3 t. chili powder
1-1/2 t. salt

1/2 t. dried oregano
1/4 t. pepper
1/8 t. hot pepper sauce
1 bay leaf
1-1/2 c. water
1 c. celery, chopped
1 c. green pepper, chopped
Garnish: shredded Cheddar
cheese and sour cream

In a Dutch oven over medium heat, brown ground beef with onion; drain. Stir in remaining ingredients except garnish. Bring to a boil; reduce heat and simmer for one hour. Cover and simmer for 10 minutes; remove bay leaf before serving. Spoon into serving bowls; garnish with cheese and sour cream.

Slow roasting or simmering works wonders on inexpensive, less-tender cuts of beef...arm and chuck roast, rump roast, short ribs, round steak and stew beef cook up juicy and delicious.

Family Swiss Steak

Makes 4 servings

1-1/2 lbs. beef round steak,
   cut into serving-size pieces
3 T. all-purpose flour
1 T. fresh parsley, chopped
1/4 t. dried thyme
1/8 t. pepper

2 T. oil
1/2 c. onion, sliced
2 carrots, peeled and cut
   in strips
10-3/4 oz. can French onion
   soup

With a meat mallet, pound steak to 1/4-inch thickness. In a pie plate, stir together flour, parsley, thyme and pepper. Coat steak with flour mixture. Heat oil in a skillet. Add steak and brown over medium heat, about 3 to 4 minutes on each side; add remaining ingredients. Reduce heat to low; cover and continue cooking for an additional 50 to 60 minutes.

When a recipe calls for olive oil, less-expensive light olive oil is just fine for cooking. Reserve extra-virgin olive oil for delicately flavored salad dressings and dipping sauces.

Chicken Pizza Pizazz

Makes 6 to 8 servings

1 loaf French bread, halved
    lengthwise
8-oz. can pizza sauce
1 c. cooked chicken, diced
1 c. zucchini, quartered
    and sliced

1/4 lb. pasteurized process
    cheese spread, cubed
1/3 c. sliced black olives
1 t. Italian seasoning

Place both halves of loaf on an ungreased baking sheet, cut-side up. Combine remaining ingredients; mix lightly. Spread each bread half with half of mixture; cover with aluminum foil. Bake at 350 degrees for 25 to 30 minutes, or until cheese is melted. Slice to serve.

For a speedy side, give a homemade taste to packaged stuffing mixes with very little effort. Sauté 1/4 cup each of chopped onion and celery, add to the stuffing mix and prepare as the package directs.

Homestyle Turkey & Stuffing   *Makes 4 to 6 servings*

2 c. cooked turkey, cubed
4 c. assorted vegetables,
     sliced into bite-size pieces
     and cooked
10-3/4 oz. can cream of celery
     soup
10-3/4 oz. can cream of potato
     soup

1 c. milk
1/4 t. dried thyme
1/8 t. pepper
4 c. prepared sage-flavored
     stuffing mix

Arrange turkey in a greased, shallow 3-quart casserole dish; top with vegetables. Stir together soups, milk, thyme and pepper in a bowl; spread over turkey and vegetables. Top with stuffing. Bake, uncovered, at 400 degrees for 25 minutes, until hot.

Canned tomatoes are economical, delicious and are even available already seasoned...that's like getting herbs and spices free! They're often a better buy than less-than-ripe fresh tomatoes.

Tomato-Beef Stew

Serves 4 to 6

4 carrots, peeled and sliced
2 stalks celery, sliced
4 potatoes, peeled and diced
1 onion, diced

1-1/2 lbs. ground beef,
   browned and drained
16-oz. can stewed tomatoes
1/2 to 1 c. red steak sauce

Place carrots, celery, potatoes and onion in a stockpot; cover with water. Boil until tender; drain. Stir in ground beef and tomatoes; add steak sauce to taste. Heat through.

Nothing goes better with hearty baked beans than warm cornbread! Bake it in a vintage cast-iron skillet...cornbread will bake up with a crisp golden crust.

Bunk House Beans

1 lb. ground beef
1/2 c. onion, chopped
15-oz. can butter beans
15-1/2 oz. can kidney beans
16-oz. can pork & beans

1 c. catsup
3/4 c. brown sugar, packed
1 t. dry mustard
1 T. vinegar

Brown beef and onion in a large skillet over medium heat; drain.
Combine beef mixture and remaining ingredients in a bowl, mixing
well. Place mixture in a greased 13"x9" baking pan. Bake, uncovered,
at 350 degrees for one hour.

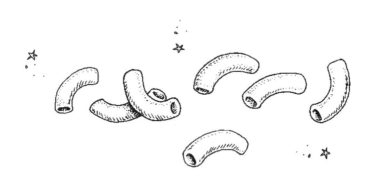

Leftover cooked pasta doesn't need to go to waste. Toss with oil, wrap tightly and refrigerate up to 4 days. To serve, place in a metal colander, dip into boiling water for one minute and drain...as good as fresh-cooked!

Tuna Pea Doodle

10-3/4 oz. can cream of
    mushroom soup
1-1/4 c. milk
3 T. butter, diced
16-oz. pkg. medium egg
    noodles, cooked

15-1/4 oz. can peas, drained
6-oz. can tuna, drained
celery salt and pepper to taste

Mix together soup, milk and butter in a large saucepan over low heat.
Gently stir in noodles, peas and tuna. Simmer until heated through,
about 10 minutes. Stir in celery salt and pepper to taste.

Soup is a "souper" way to save on meals! Why not serve soup
once a week...just add a basket of warm bread for a satisfying,
thrifty dinner that everyone is sure to enjoy.

Vermont Potato Soup

Makes 6 servings

1 c. onion, chopped
1 clove garlic, minced
3 T. butter
4 c. chicken broth
4 potatoes, cubed
2 T. fresh parsley, chopped

salt and pepper to taste
8-oz. pkg. shredded Cheddar
   cheese
Garnish: 4 slices bacon, crisply
   cooked and crumbled, and
   3/4 c. croutons, crushed

Combine onions, garlic and butter in a Dutch oven and cook over medium heat for 5 minutes. Blend in chicken broth, potatoes, parsley, salt and pepper to taste. Simmer, covered, for 20 minutes then remove from heat. Spoon mixture into a food processor and purée small amounts at a time. Return to Dutch oven and stir in Cheddar cheese; heat through. Combine bacon and croutons; sprinkle over soup before serving.

Spread saltines with softened butter, then sprinkle with garlic salt, paprika or another favorite seasoning. Pop into a 350-degree oven just until golden, 3 to 6 minutes.

New England Fish Chowder

Makes 6 servings

1 T. oil
1/2 c. onion, chopped
2-1/2 c. potatoes, peeled and
　　diced
1-1/2 c. boiling water
salt and pepper to taste

1 lb. frozen cod or haddock
　　fillets, thawed and cut into
　　large chunks
2 c. milk
1 T. butter

Heat oil in a large saucepan. Add onion; cook over medium heat until tender. Add potatoes, water, salt and pepper. Reduce heat; cover and simmer for 15 to 20 minutes, until potatoes are tender. Add fish; simmer until fish flakes easily, about 5 minutes. Just before serving, add milk and butter; heat through.

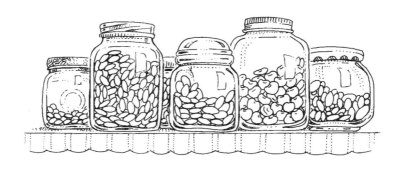

Dried beans and peas are healthful, delicious, come in lots
of varieties and cost just pennies per serving...what more
could you ask for? Store them in canning jars on the kitchen
counter for farmhouse-kitchen style.

Hearty Bean Soup

Makes 10 servings

16-oz. pkg. dried Great
   Northern beans
1 meaty ham bone
1/2 c. onion, chopped
1/2 c. celery with leaves,
   chopped

salt and pepper to taste
Garnish: additional chopped
   onion

Cover beans with water; soak overnight. Drain and rinse beans; place in a large soup pot with remaining ingredients except garnish. Add water to cover. Cook over medium heat for one hour, until ham is falling off the bone. Remove bone and dice ham; return ham to pot. Continue cooking until beans are tender, about 2 hours. Garnish with additional chopped onion.

Give any chunky veggie soup a creamier texture...no cream
required! Use a hand-held immersion blender to purée
some of the cooked veggies right in the saucepan.

Cream of Broccoli Soup

1 bunch broccoli, chopped
1 onion, chopped
4 c. chicken broth
4 T. butter

1/2 c. all-purpose flour
2 c. milk
salt, pepper and garlic powder
    to taste

Simmer broccoli and onion in broth in a large stockpot over medium heat until tender, about 10 to 12 minutes. In a separate saucepan, melt butter over medium heat; whisk in flour. Add milk; cook, stirring constantly, until thickened. Whisk milk mixture into broccoli mixture; reduce heat and simmer for 5 to 10 additional minutes.

Instead of soft drinks, serve oh-so-easy iced tea with meals.
Fill a 2-quart pitcher with water and drop in 6 to 8 teabags.
Refrigerate overnight. Discard teabags and add ice cubes
and sugar to taste...cool and refreshing!

Seasoned Potato Wedges

Makes 4 servings

4 russet potatoes   2 t. seasoned salt
2-1/2 T. mayonnaise

Cut potatoes in half lengthwise; cut each half into 3 wedges. Place in
a single layer on a greased baking sheet. Spread mayonnaise over cut
sides of potatoes; sprinkle with seasoned salt. Bake at 350 degrees for
50 to 60 minutes, or until tender.

Copy tried & true recipes onto file cards and have them laminated at a copying store. Punch a hole in the upper left corner and thread cards onto a key ring...now you can tuck them in your purse, ready for any shopping trip!

Baked Chiles Rellenos

Serves 4

7-oz. can whole green chiles, drained
1/2 lb. sharp Cheddar cheese

2 eggs, beaten
1/2 c. all-purpose flour
1-1/2 c. milk

Slice chiles down the center; arrange in a lightly buttered
13"x9" baking pan and set aside. Slice cheese to fit inside chiles;
place in chiles. Whisk egg, flour and milk together; pour over chiles.
Bake, uncovered, at 350 degrees for 45 to 50 minutes.

Don't pass up a good deal on overripe produce! Past-their-prime
zucchini, yellow squash, mushrooms, eggplant and sweet potatoes
are scrumptious sliced and roasted with a drizzle of olive oil.

Italian Green Beans

Serves 4

2 14-1/2 oz. cans green beans   1 t. Italian seasoning
1/2 c. Italian salad dressing

Place beans in a medium saucepan; stir in salad dressing and
seasoning. Bring to a boil over medium heat; turn down to a simmer.
Cook, stirring occasionally, until most of liquid is gone.

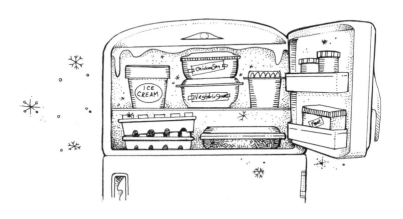

Keep a couple of favorite side dishes on hand in the freezer to make spur-of-the-moment dinners easy. Pair them with grilled meats or a deli roast chicken for a hearty meal in a hurry.

Maple-Glazed Carrots

Serves 4

16-oz. pkg. baby carrots
3 slices bacon, chopped
1 apple, cored, peeled and sliced
   into thin wedges

2 T. maple syrup
salt and pepper to taste

Place carrots in a saucepan and cover with water; bring to a boil over medium heat. Cook for 10 minutes, or until crisp-tender; drain. Set aside. Cook bacon in a skillet over medium heat for 3 minutes, or until lightly browned. Add apple and cook for 2 minutes. Add carrots, maple syrup, salt and pepper; stir frequently. Cook until carrots are warmed through and lightly glazed. Serve immediately.

Everybody loves fried rice! With this recipe you can turn leftover cooked rice into a tasty side in a jiffy. Toss in leftover peas and carrots too...even chopped cooked chicken or pork to turn it into a satisfying main dish.

Oriental Fried Rice

Makes 4 servings

2 T. oil
3-1/2 c. cooked rice, chilled
2 T. soy sauce

1/4 c. green onions, thinly
    sliced
1 egg, beaten

Heat a non-stick skillet or wok. Add oil and heat over medium heat until just smoking. Carefully add rice; stir in soy sauce and onions. Cook and stir for 5 minutes. Add egg; cook and stir just until egg has cooked through.

Baked tomatoes are a tasty garnish for grilled meats. Cut ripe
tomatoes in half, dot with butter, then sprinkle with grated
Parmesan cheese and oregano. Bake at 425 degrees
for 10 to 15 minutes.

Grilled Parmesan Potatoes

6 potatoes, peeled and thinly
　　sliced
1 onion, thinly sliced
1/2 c. grated Parmesan cheese

2 cloves garlic, minced
4 T. butter, cubed
1 t. seasoning salt
1/2 t. pepper

Layer 2 pieces of aluminum foil about 20 inches long. Combine all ingredients in a bowl; mix well. Place potato mixture in the center of the aluminum foil; fold foil up around potatoes and seal. Grill, covered, over medium heat for 30 to 40 minutes, or until potatoes are tender. Packet may also be placed on a baking sheet; bake at 450 degrees for 35 minutes.

Shake up a simple dressing for tossed salads! In a small jar, combine 2 tablespoons cider vinegar, 6 tablespoons olive oil in a small jar and salt and pepper to taste. Twist on the lid and shake well.

Mother's Cucumber Salad

Serves 6

3 to 4 cucumbers, peeled and
thinly sliced
3 T. salt
2 t. sugar
1/2 t. onion powder

1/4 t. celery seed
1/4 t. pepper
1/4 c. cider vinegar
Optional: 1/2 c. sliced red onion

Place cucumbers in a large bowl; add salt and enough water to cover.
Cover and shake to mix salt. Refrigerate several hours to overnight.
Drain cucumbers, but do not rinse; return to bowl. Stir together sugar,
onion powder, celery seed, pepper and vinegar; mix well. Pour
vinegar mixture over top of cucumbers. Add onion, if desired. Cover
and shake gently to mix.

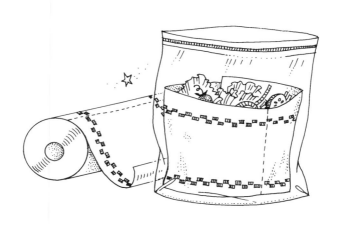

Keep salad greens fresh longer. Wrap in paper towels to absorb
moisture, seal in a plastic zipping bag and tuck into the crisping
drawer of the refrigerator.

Simply Coleslaw

Serves 6

1 head cabbage, chopped
4 carrots, peeled and grated
1 onion, chopped
8-oz. can sliced pineapple,
    drained and chopped

8-oz. container plain
    low-fat yogurt
salt and pepper to taste
Optional: garlic powder and
    paprika to taste

In a large serving bowl, mix cabbage, carrots, onion, pineapple and yogurt. Add salt and pepper to taste; if desired, add garlic powder and paprika. Chill for 30 minutes before serving.

Check out what's new at the supermarket! You just may find an old favorite in a new flavor to spice up a tried & true recipe...cream soups, shredded cheese blends and salad dressings, just to name a few.

Sweet-and-Sour Dressing

Makes 10 servings

6 T. cider vinegar
1 c. brown sugar, packed
1 T. sugar

1/4 c. oil
1/4 t. garlic salt

In a small saucepan over low heat, cook and stir all ingredients until sugars are dissolved. Cool; pour into a covered container. May be kept refrigerated for up to 2 weeks.

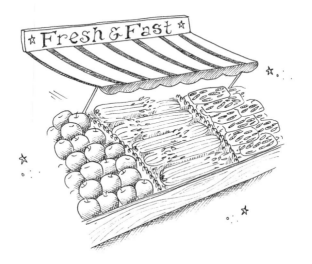

Choose local, seasonal fresh fruits and vegetables instead of
ones that have been shipped a long distance. You'll be serving
your family the freshest, tastiest produce year 'round
at the lowest prices.

Green Pea Salad

4 slices bacon, crisply cooked
    and crumbled
3 green onions, sliced
1 stalk celery, diced
10-oz. pkg. frozen peas, thawed

1/4 c. mayonnaise
1/4 c. sour cream
1/4 t. salt
1/8 t. pepper

Combine all ingredients together in a serving bowl. Chill before serving.

Keep bags of sweetened dried cranberries and chopped walnuts
tucked in the cupboard for healthy between-meal snacking.
A quick toss of nuts & berries really dresses up a
plain-Jane salad in a snap too.

Eric's Favorite Sauce

Makes about 1-1/4 cups

1/2 c. canola oil
1/4 c. red wine vinegar
1/4 c. creamy peanut butter

1/4 c. honey
1 t. Dijon mustard
1/4 t. salt

Combine all ingredients in a jar; cover and shake until well blended.
Store in refrigerator. To use, drizzle over salad greens or serve as a dip
with cut-up vegetables.

If you're making biscuits and don't have a biscuit cutter handy,
a glass tumbler or the open end of a clean, empty soup can
will work just as well.

Anytime Cheesy Biscuits

Makes about 1-1/2 dozen

2 c. biscuit baking mix
1/2 c. shredded Cheddar cheese
2/3 c. milk

1/4 c. margarine, melted
1/4 t. garlic powder

Combine first 3 ingredients together until a soft dough forms; beat vigorously for 30 seconds. Drop dough by rounded tablespoonfuls onto an ungreased baking sheet. Bake at 450 degrees until golden, about 8 to 10 minutes. Whisk margarine and garlic powder together; spread over warm biscuits.

Don't toss that lemon or orange half after it's been juiced! Wrap it and store in the freezer, ready to grate whenever a recipe calls for fresh citrus zest.

Lemon Bread

Makes one loaf

1-1/2 c. all-purpose flour
1 t. baking powder
1/2 t. salt
6 T. shortening
1-1/3 c. sugar, divided

2 eggs, beaten
1 T. lemon zest
1/2 c. milk
3 T. lemon juice

Mix together flour, baking powder and salt; set aside. Blend together shortening and one cup sugar; add eggs and lemon zest. Stir into flour mixture alternately with milk. Pour into a greased and floured 8-1/2"x4-1/2" loaf pan. Bake at 350 degrees for one hour, or until center tests done. Dissolve remaining sugar in lemon juice; drizzle over bread. Remove from pan to cool.

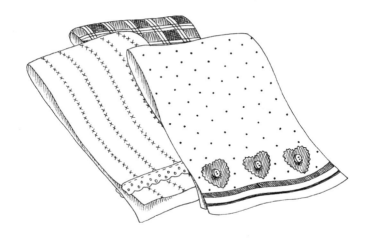

Cotton tea towels are oh-so handy in the kitchen. They're reusable too...much thriftier than paper towels! Look for vintage tea towels at tag sales, or dress up plain towels by stitching on brightly colored rick rack.

Parmesan Bread Sticks

Makes one dozen

1/3 c. butter, melted
1 t. dried rosemary
1 clove garlic, minced
2-1/4 c. all-purpose flour

2 T. grated Parmesan cheese
1 T. sugar
3-1/2 t. baking powder
1 c. milk

Pour butter into a 13"x9" baking pan tilting to coat; sprinkle with rosemary and garlic. Set aside. Combine flour, cheese, sugar and baking powder; stir in milk. Turn dough onto a floured surface; knead until smooth. Roll into a 12"x6" rectangle; cut into one-inch strips. Twist each strip 6 times; place in butter mixture. Bake at 400 degrees for 20 to 25 minutes, until golden. Serve warm.

Honey butter is delectable melting into warm biscuits. Simply blend
2/3 cup honey with 1/2 cup softened butter.

Fluffy Whole-Wheat Biscuits *Makes one dozen*

1 c. all-purpose flour
1 c. whole-wheat flour
4 t. baking powder
1 T. sugar

3/4 t. salt
1/4 c. butter
1 c. milk

Combine flours, baking powder, sugar and salt; mix well. Cut in butter until mixture resembles coarse crumbs. Stir in milk just until moistened. Turn dough out onto a lightly floured surface; knead gently 8 to 10 times. Roll out to 3/4-inch thickness. Cut with a 2-1/2" round biscuit cutter. Place biscuits on an ungreased baking sheet. Bake at 450 degrees for 10 to 12 minutes, or until lightly golden. Serve warm.

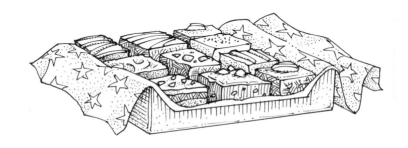

Save bottom-of-the-box leftovers of crunchy breakfast cereal
in a canister to use in a favorite crunchy treat recipe. Chewy
Cereal Bars or marshmallow crispy treats will be
just as yummy, and you'll be saving money!

Chewy Cereal Bars

Makes 2 to 2-1/2 dozen

1 c. sugar
1 c. light corn syrup
1 c. creamy peanut butter

1 t. vanilla extract
6 c. doughnut-shaped oat cereal

Stir together sugar and corn syrup in a saucepan over medium heat; boil for one minute. Remove from heat; add peanut butter and vanilla, stirring until smooth. Place cereal in a large bowl coated with non-stick cooking spray; stir in peanut butter mixture. Press into a buttered 15"x10" jelly-roll pan and let cool. Slice into squares.

Big glasses of icy cold milk are a must with homemade cookies!
Save by using instant non-fat powdered milk. For the tastiest
flavor, add a little vanilla extract and chill the milk
overnight before serving.

Soft Peanut Butter Cookies

Makes 2 to 3 dozen

1 c. sugar
1 c. creamy peanut butter

1 egg, beaten
1 t. vanilla extract

Combine all ingredients; mix well. Drop by teaspoonfuls onto a
baking sheet; use a fork to press a criss-cross pattern on top of each
cookie. Bake at 325 degrees for 10 minutes, or until golden. Let cool
before removing from baking sheet.

Bread pudding is a scrumptious way to use up day-old bread.
Try French bread, raisin bread or even leftover cinnamon
buns or doughnuts for an extra-tasty dessert!

Annie's Bread Pudding

Makes 6 to 8 servings

1/4 c. butter
3/4 t. ground ginger
1/2 t. cinnamon
1/4 t. salt
8 slices bread

1/2 c. raisins
4 eggs, beaten
1/4 c. honey
1/4 c. brown sugar
4 c. milk

Blend first 4 ingredients together until fluffy. Spread each bread slice with butter mixture; layer with raisins in a greased 9"x5" loaf pan. Combine eggs, honey, brown sugar and milk in a large bowl and pour over bread; allow to stand 15 to 20 minutes. Place loaf pan in another baking pan filled half full with water. Bake at 325 degrees for one hour, or until a knife inserted in center comes out clean.

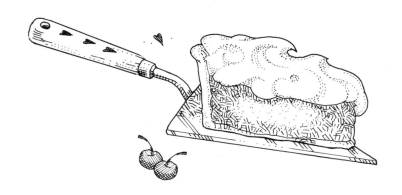

Make your own crumb crusts. Combine 1-1/2 cups finely crushed graham crackers, vanilla wafers or chocolate cookies, 1/4 cup sugar and 1/2 cup melted butter. Mix well and press into a pie plate. Bake at 350 degrees for 10 minutes, cool and fill as desired.

Mom's Cherry Cream Pie

Makes 8 servings

1/2 pt. whipping cream
1/2 c. powdered sugar
3-oz. pkg. cream cheese,
    softened

9-inch pie crust, baked
21-oz. can cherry pie filling

In a bowl, blend whipping cream, powdered sugar and cream cheese
together until smooth. Spoon into cooled pie crust and top with pie
filling; chill until set.

Grease and flour cake pans in one easy step. Combine 1/2 cup
shortening with 1/4 cup all-purpose flour. Keep this handy mix
in a covered container at room temperature.

Sweet & Simple Comfort Cake

Serves 8 to 10

1 c. sugar
1 c. all-purpose flour
1 t. baking soda
1/8 t. salt
15-oz. can fruit cocktail,
    drained

1 egg, beaten
3/4 c. brown sugar, packed
1/2 c. chopped nuts
Garnish: whipped topping

In a bowl, sift sugar, flour, baking soda and salt together; stir in fruit cocktail and egg. Mix well; pour into a greased 13"x9" baking pan. Sprinkle with brown sugar and nuts; bake at 350 degrees for 45 minutes. Let cool; top with whipped cream.

Whip up cake-mix cookies for a quick treat! Blend together a
9-ounce package of favorite-flavor cake mix with one beaten
egg, one tablespoon melted shortening and 2 tablespoons water.
Drop by teaspoonfuls onto a greased baking sheet and bake
at 350 degrees for 10 minutes. Makes 2 dozen.

Magic Fudge Cake

Makes 12 servings

18-1/2 oz. pkg. chocolate fudge
   cake mix

12-oz. can regular or diet cola
Garnish: whipped topping

Combine dry cake mix and cola in a large bowl. Stir until well
blended. Pour batter into a 13"x9" baking pan that has been
sprayed with non-stick vegetable spray. Bake at 350 degrees for
35 minutes, or until cake pulls away from sides of pan. Cool; top with
whipped topping.

Head out to a pick-your-own apple orchard for a day of fresh-air fun. The kids will love it, and you'll come home with bushels of the best-tasting apples for applesauce, cobblers and crisps!

Easy Apple Crisp

Makes 6 servings

6 baking apples, cored, peeled
   and sliced
1/2 c. butter, melted
3/4 c. brown sugar, packed

3/4 c. quick-cooking oats,
   uncooked
1/2 c. all-purpose flour
1/2 t. cinnamon

Place apples into a buttered 11"x7" baking pan. In a bowl, combine
remaining ingredients; sprinkle over apples. Bake at 350 degrees
until apples are soft, about 35 minutes.

INDEX

INDEX

Our Story

Back in 1984, we were next-door neighbors raising our families in the little town of Delaware, Ohio. We were two moms with small children looking for a way to do what we loved and stay home with the kids too. We shared a love of home cooking and making memories with family & friends. After many a conversation over the backyard fence, **Gooseberry Patch** was born.

We put together the first catalog & cookbooks at our kitchen tables and packed boxes from the basement, enlisting the help of our loved ones wherever we could. From that little family, we've grown to include an amazing group of creative folks who love cooking, decorating and creating as much as we do.

Hard to believe it's been over 25 years since those kitchen-table days. Today, we're best known for our homestyle, family-friendly cookbooks. We love hand-picking the recipes and are tickled to share our inspiration, ideas and more with you! One thing's for sure, we couldn't have done it without our friends all across the country. Whether you've been along for the ride from the beginning or are just discovering us, welcome to our family!

Vickie & JoAnn

Want to hear the latest from **Gooseberry Patch**?
www.gooseberrypatch.com

Join Our Circle of Friends

VIDEOS

Read Our Blog

Find us on Facebook

Follow us on twitter

1·800·854·6673